Jaan Kaplinski

The Wandering Border

The Wandering Border

POEMS BY JAAN KAPLINSKI

TRANSLATED FROM THE ESTONIAN BY THE AUTHOR
WITH SAM HAMILL AND RIINA TAMM

COPPER CANYON PRESS : PORT TOWNSEND

ISBN : 1-55659-009-1 (CLOTH)

ISBN : 1-55659-010-5 (PAPER)

LIBRARY OF CONGRESS CATALOG NUMBER : 87-71141

A number of these poems were first published in
American Poetry Review, Willow Springs, and in
the anthology *Borderlands,* edited by John Ellison
(Broken Moon Press).

The publication of this book was supported by a grant
from the National Endowment for the Arts.

Copper Canyon Press is in residence with Centrum
at Fort Worden State Park.

COPPER CANYON PRESS

P.O. Box 271

Port Townsend, Washington 98368

TABLE OF CONTENTS

PART

I

THE EAST-WEST BORDER is always wandering,
sometimes eastward, sometimes west,
and we do not know exactly where it is just now:
in Gaugamela, in the Urals, or maybe in ourselves,
so that one ear, one eye, one nostril, one hand, one foot,
one lung and one testicle or one ovary
is on the one, another on the other side. Only the heart,
only the heart is always on one side:
if we are looking northward, in the West;
if we are looking southward, in the East;
and the mouth doesn't know on behalf of which or both
it has to speak.

I COULD HAVE SAID: I stepped from the bus.
I stood on the dusty roadside where
a young maple and dog-roses grew.
But really, I leaped into the silence,
and there was no land, no surface to step on.
The silence closed over my head:
I saw how the bus had just departed,
and sinking deeper and deeper
I heard only my own heart beating,
and in the rhythm of it, I saw my own street
passing with all its well-known signs:
lilies-of-the-valley and Equiseti Silvestres,
Oxalis nearly in flower,
an anthill covered by a brownish ripple –
the ants themselves. The Big Pine. The Big Spruce.
Stackpoles. The Sandhole. The fireplace.
The white trunks of birch trees. The Big Stone.
And many memories. Silence, the inland sea, –
what else could I name for you?

THIS SUMMER is full of insects.
As soon as you go to the garden,
a cloud of flies buzzes around your head.
Bumblebees nest in the birdhouses,
wasps nest in the hazel,
and as I sit at the window
I hear a buzz I cannot name,
whether the voice of bumblebees, wasps,
or electric lines,
a plane in the sky, a car on the road,
or the voice of life itself that wants
to tell you something from the inside out.

From childhood on, I have scribbled on paper –
bowie knives, pistols, men's faces.
Now, one afternoon, I suddenly noticed
I had begun to draw
cats, dogs, horses, and birds.
Although clumsily, with anatomical faults,
but if I continue,
they will perhaps improve,
become more real, more alive,
and, who knows, perhaps even sometime
move, even stretch themselves
or lift their wings
from grayish paper, from between
poems and lecture notes, as once, long ago,
a yellow crane drawn by a student
on a teahouse wall.

THE WASHING never gets done.
The furnace never gets heated.
Books never get read.
Life is never completed.
Life is like a ball which one must continually
catch and hit so that it won't fall.
When the fence is repaired at one end,
it collapses at the other. The roof leaks,
the kitchen door won't close, there are cracks in the foundation,
the torn knees of children's pants . . .
One can't keep everything in mind. The wonder is
that beside all this one can notice
the spring which is so full of everything
continuing in all directions – into evening clouds,
into the redwing's song and into every
drop of dew on every blade of grass in the meadow,
as far as the eye can see, into the dusk.

My WIFE AND CHILDREN were waiting for ice cream.
For a while, I had nothing else to do
but stand, looking underfoot:
Festuca, Poa, Trifolium repens, Taraxacum vulgare
and just on the edge of the sidewalk, where people
often pass hurrying from the market hall to the bus station,
it's you, Potentilla anserina, an old acquaintance
from Tartumaa and Võrumaa farmyards
we can never forget as we cannot also forget
gooseshit I so often stepped in
and that stuck between my toes.

We STARTED HOME, my son and I.
Twilight already. The young moon
stood in the western sky and beside it
a single star. I showed them to my son
and explained how the moon should be greeted
and that this star is the moon's servant.
As we neared home, he said
that the moon is far, as far
as that place where we went.
I told him the moon is much, much farther
and reckoned: if one were to walk
ten kilometers each day, it would take
almost a hundred years to reach the moon.
But this was not what he wanted to hear.
The road was already almost dry.
The river was spread on the marsh; ducks and other waterfowl
crowed the beginning of night. The snow's crust
crackled underfoot – it must
have been freezing again. All the houses' windows
were dark. Only in our kitchen
a light shone. Beside our chimney, the shining moon,
and beside the moon, a single star.

THERE WAS WINTER'S COLD and moisture
in the bedclothes, in the walls and floor,
our bodies tired from a long day's work.
At night I dreamt I caught the two yellow ducklings,
and struggled to keep my hold.
It was easiest keeping them in my breast pockets.
I wanted to bring them home to raise them,
but realized then I didn't know what
to feed them. I don't remember the rest.
I probably went to the opera, but this
may have been a dream from the night before.
In the morning, weeding flowerbeds,
Tiia found a little hare crouching under a poppy.

My little daughter, with both her hands, is strewing
white sawdust on white birchbark.
The wind is blowing from the southwest. Everything
is suddenly so full of this wind
and of this autumn. It is as if
the movement of the clouds has
at last moved something that until now
did not stir, was in blossom, was lush and green. Everywhere
such clarity that oblivion finds no place.
Barberries on thorny twigs.
Nettles near the barn door already yellow.
But the birchbark and the fresh sawdust
under the saw and in the tiny palm of the child
suddenly so much more white and clean than before.

To WRITE MORE. To speak more. To whom?
How? Why? What sense does it make? Soon
we may be forced into silence. Soon
we may be forced to speak more
and more loudly. Who knows. But what
remains unspoken is always the most important:
this little man, this child, this
word, thought, and look of a child
deep inside you, you must guard,
you must defend and cherish.
And with it you will learn to speak,
and with it you will learn to be silent
if you must.

O<small>N THE OTHER SIDE</small> of the window,
    on the other side of the pylon,
of the dung barrow and snowberry bush,
on the other side of the barn roof where southwest wind
for the third day is scattering ash leaves;
on the other side of the Crincels apple tree,
of the raspberries and of the spruce hedge,
on the other side of the foggy field, of the forest and clouds,
of the autumn, of the sky, of the wind,
on the other side of this life, here,
suddenly, a lone tardy dandelion
unfolds and takes
thoughts from my head and words from my mouth.

THERE IS NO GOOD, no Evil, no Sin, no Virtue,
no Faithfulness, no Unfaithfulness, no Marriage, no Adultery.
There is also no Love, although sometimes
these and other words are spoken or written
on paper, on sand, into stone or wind.
There is only the great soul which has
no greatness nor smallness, something
between thoughts and entrails that sometimes starts
as I see you gathering apples under an apple tree
or cutting our little boy's hair or taking
off your nightgown, and I do not know
whether the echo of this beginning will ever end.

PART

II

THE WIND SWAYS the lilac branches and shadows
come through the open porch door onto the floor
and also sway. Today I washed the windows
and was sad a long while: all at once everything was
so close, so visible, so right here,
that my own distance stood out still more,
inconsolably. Is it really that
only in the autumn wood, in the company of titmice and spruce,
I have been with my own? With myself?
                         And from where, this sadness?
The sun rolls on. The wind dies down.
Lilac branches' shadows sway on the bookshelf
and are gone.

THIS MORNING was cold, but it warmed about mid-day.
Blue clouds piled up in the north.
I came from a meeting – a discussion of
the teaching of classical languages –
and I was sitting by the river with a friend
who wanted to tell me his troubles.
The water was still high. Two boys
were throwing pebbles from the bank into the river.
I had no counsel to offer.... There were
no benches on the bank – probably night vandals
had thrown them into the water once again.
The sun slipped behind a cloud. We were freezing.
We rose and went back to town.
Perhaps he could see his course.
I stopped at a shop for oatmeal and bread.
It was June. Going home, I saw
three young militiamen winding their Rubik's cube.

FOUR-AND-A-HALF TONS of Silesian coal –
a whole day to shovel it into the cellar,
a whole winter to burn it. I'm happy to have it,
and – as always – I regret a little
that I must burn something so wonderful
without having time to study it, to open layer by layer
the book that has been buried and hidden for so long.
I understand almost nothing of these
single lumps that bear distinct
traces of leaves or bark from ancient trees.
Always a book, a black book in a foreign language
from which I understand only some single words:
Cordaites, Bennetites, Sigillaria, Sigillaria . . .

ONCE WHILE carrying coal ash and used paint
　　　drums to the dustbin
I remembered it once more: there is
no difference between the common and the strange.
If there is any difference, it is only in ourselves, in our eyes.
For God, it is as common to create or to destroy worlds
as it is for us to write a letter or to read
editorials or the obit page. To himself,
God is no God. To ourselves, we are gods.
In this sense, there is no God. There are
eyes, eyes where a rusty oil barrel takes tender white roots,
and yesterday's newspaper bursts into bloom
and moths swarm around it till dawn.

I DO NOT KNOW whether each believer
is as joyful that God exists
as I was upon hearing
the wood owl call from the ash tree
where his nest box
has already rested a dozen years. Now
he has nested there
four or five years himself.
He is.

NIGHT COMES, and the children sleep.
Silence returns from I-don't-know-where –
probably from deep below and from high above.
The silence rings in the ears.
White Tara's smile on the postcard
is clearer and the colors around her
brighter. I will linger at this smile
and write a few lines. From these lines,
I live, in some sense, after all.
From this smile (in another sense) also.

P EOPLE were coming from the market carrying plum trees;
white lines were being drawn on the asphalt.
Going home, I saw once more
the white tortured trunks of birches
and their foliage breaking out in leaves
and the clouded sky reflected in floodwater pools,
I suddenly felt that this beauty
was becoming almost unsupportable –
it's better to look on ground where charming
tiny burdocks, nettles, and mugworts
are coming up
or go indoors and find in the dictionaries
what, after all, are the meanings of Japanese words,
yugen, sabi, and *mono-no-aware*:
obscurity, mystery,
and charm or sadness for what is.

THE GLOW OF THE NIGHT SKY –
so bright and mild that when I dip
the pail into the well, I see
my own face clearly there.
But the water I draw out
is always the same: liquid,
cold, colorless, tasteless, odorless.

SOMETIMES I SEE so clearly the openness of things.
The teapot has no lid, the colt has no saddle.
Black horses come racing out of memory
carrying young boys on their backs and rush over
the empty steppe and through the haze
through which we see, dimly,
some single peaks. . . . I too have come from there.
I have something of you, my forefathers,
Amurat, Ahmed, Tokhtash, something of you
black Tartar horses on boundless expanses.
I too do not like to return
to lived life, to an extinguished fire,
to a thought thought to a written poem.
I am burning with the same urge to reach the Atlantic,
to reach the borders always vanishing and breaking
in front of the black horses who again and again
race out from memories and steppes
smelling the west wind that brings from somewhere very far
the odor of the sea and rain.

I DON'T EVEN KNOW if I have the right to say "green" –
I'm a Daltonian and I don't see this color . . .
I don't know what to say of this forest floor
that suddenly burst into colors, became a microcosm
amidst the evening dusk in late autumn:
bright moss, lush and luxuriant, now
in the damp cold after a summer drought.
Some cowberry stalks, a pine cone, a May lily,
some yellow pine needles, some little twigs and sprigs –
all of them heavy, as if
this silence and this dusk oozed into them
and stopped everything in a bottomless immobility
where a single heartbeat must wait endlessly for another,
and two needles fall eternally
from the pine.

THE SUN HAS RISEN. The wind has risen.
In fact, it blew the night through from the west
between the windows. The river
has also risen, the ditches
are overflowing. On the meadow
this side of the willow thicket, the dawn sky shimmers
with hurrying clouds and clamoring gulls.
Time begins to flow again. The curtain at the window
floats softly. I try to count
my breaths: one, two, three, four,
five, six, ... But always, before I reach ten,
thought has slid away into something else,
as if knowing how good it is to excuse
oneself with spring. But why? And to whom?

PART

III

It gets cold in the evening. The sky clears.
The wind dies out, and the smoke
rises straight up. The flowering maple
no longer buzzes. A carp
plops in the pond. An owl hoots twice
in its nest in the ash tree.
The children are asleep. On the stairs,
a long row of shoes and rubber boots.
It happened near Viljandi: an imbecile boy
poured gasoline on the neighbor's three-year-old son
and set him on fire. I ran for milk.
You could see the yellow maple from far off
between the birches and the spruce. The evening star
was shining above the storehouse. The boy survived,
probably maimed for life. The night will bring frost.
Plentiful dew.

A PIEBALD CAT
sits alone in the middle of the mown field
waiting for something, perhaps a mouse,
perhaps for darkness. We all
wait for the rain. Clouds came and went;
in the morning, it drizzled, but then the wind rose
and raged until noon, drying
even that scant moisture. The village people
grumble that their cattle have hardly anything to eat.
Time moves sideways, looking at this
empty land above which
warm south winds sweep and buzzards
shriek. No longer summer. Nor autumn yet.

THE EARLY AUTUMN, a faded aquarelle,
becoming more and more colorless and depthless.
Big clumsy flies creeping through window slits
into our rooms, unable to get out again,
as every autumn. From evening to evening,
clouds gather, but there is no dew at night. Jays
pick last peas in the garden.
Thrushes perch in flocks on rowan trees.
Everything seen and known before. The long drought
leaves its traces in our face and mind,
and it is difficult to believe that there is something new
under the sun save the wind and deceptive clouds,
meteor flashes in the night sky and some
chance things you happen to see and remember as with this
earwig that for a long while was turning around
on the gravel path in front of our house.

THE CROP IS REAPED and mice are coming in from the fields
to the farmhouse, and the owls follow them in.
Sometimes in the evening they call one another
from one corner of the garden to another. I found
a butterfly with worn-out wings in the grass – it could not
fly any more. One night while I went out to pee,
I saw the Milky Way for the first time. A nutcracker
shrieked in the hazel hedge – the nuts are ripe.
The wasps abandoned their nests. They are flying
and feasting, slipping into beehives,
into jam cans and overripe apples;
and grasshoppers are sawing in the grass and on the trees
more and more loudly, and dolorous
as the summer's last string knowing it will break.

POETRY IS VERDANT – in spring
it is born from each raindrop, each
ray of light falling on the ground.
How much room do we have for them
between a morning and an evening
or upon a page in a book?
But now, in autumn when black clouds
slide low above us, brushing
high-tension pylons and crows
dozing there in the dusk, because
there is hardly day at all, the night is
two long black fingers holding day
and us in a grip so tight we barely have
room to breathe or think. Everything I write
is in spite of this weight
that comes, comes again, wanting
to plunge us into sleep,
into the dreams of decaying leaves and grassroots
and of the earth itself where
all our unthought thoughts and unborn poems hide.

S ILENCE OF NIGHT. A cockroach
comes out from under the bathtub
in a fifteenth story flat; the switch
is out of order, and the lamp
often lights itself.
It climbs up the wall and stops
on the shelf just above the sink. Who knows why.
Perhaps the smell of odors oozing
from bottles, gallipots, and tubes with inscriptions
Wars After Shave Spartacus Sans Soucis Bocage
Arcancil Exotic Intim Desodor Pound's Cream
Cocoa Butter Pond's Dry Skin Cream Maquimat
Avon Chic Privileg Fath de Fath Aramis
Savon Ambre Ancien eau de Cologne . . .
Perhaps it has an inkling of something
great and mysterious, of a transcendental reality
behind these colorful labels or perhaps
the odors have simply obliterated other traces of smell
from its path leading into the socket hole and from there
into the kitchen behind the breadbox.

KNOWLEDGE HAS ALWAYS MEANT
less to me than coming to know,
than understanding. This is like fire,
the fireline moving forward along the ground,
behind ash, before last year's dried grasses,

                      last winter's mugwort
nettle stalks. Fire which always
and only rises up and moves forward.
It is like this: that the sky is
above and below and right here (even we
live in the sky). That the earth is round,
that the room is as outside of us as inside.
One grows accustomed to all this; then
knowledge is like ash. But there probably
are better metaphors: burning bog,
burning mine where fire continues for years
deep beneath the earth. . . . And also
this – what I say to others quickens, re-ignites.
Coming to know is almost making known,
understanding, giving an account, the question, the answer.
From this I understood that he
who has learned cannot be untaught.

WE ALWAYS LIVE our childhood again.
Even then, we don't want it back.
Like me. In each year-before-last's memory
is something melancholy and oppressive, probably
war and oppression's shadow from which it was so difficult,
almost impossible to get free, and still
some hazy sadness. I believe that only as a man
have I known joy, and only then,
when I began to write, the mist cleared away
and these shadows. Even from memory,
the essential is born pure:
air, water, earth, trees and houses,
and old walkway slabs on streets in suburbia
poured from concrete or cut from flat, natural stone.
Neither the eyes nor the soles of the feet have forgotten them,
and when I see them again, they are cold and soft
and pedestrians' feet have pressed them still further into a slope
so that with a child's carriage or crutches
it is already difficult to travel
Jaama, Liiva, or Tähtvere streets.
What will become of them? Will anyone
make them neatly level again,
or will they be covered with asphalt, and wheels
roll more easily over our childhood
paths and memories.

DIALECTICS IS A DIALOGUE, a play of shadows
with somebody darker than darkness
whose eye sees nothing and whose ear hears nothing.
Only sometimes it stretches its hand,
as dark as itself and imperceptibly soft,
and scatters all our cards and pieces,
our formulae, theories, religion and atheism,
and we must begin anew,
until its hand or breath once again
overturns everything
or understand that it is
permanent otherness, nothing but Something Else.

PART

I V

SPRING HAS COME indeed: willows are
         flowering and she-bumblebees
are looking for nesting places; over the bowl with sour milk
drosophilae circle; on the kitchen curtain,
just on the red speckle, a moth sleeps.
A gnat flew into the cellar chamber and buzzed around my head.
Sitting at the desk, I heard for some time
a strange rustle from a plastic envelope hanging on the wall.
At last, I took it and looked: a spider
had fallen in and was desperately trying to get out.

Destruktivität ist das Ergebnis ungelebten Lebens.
Destructivity is the result of an unlived life.
What cannot grow up grows down –
nails and hairs of the beard into the flesh, unrequited desires
calcifying our blood vessels, envy
changing into ulcers, sadness into lice,
dirt into flies. We are always,
in a way, wandering knights; we are always looking
for what to fight for and against, whom
to hate with a just hatred. This unlived life
is like a boiling water pot in our hands
which we hurry to put away, and there
is no time for anything else, and we are angry
at all who sit quietly
around the kitchen table and talk
about Erich Fromm and that destructivity
is the result of an unlived life.

THE SUN SHINES on the red wall and the wall is warm.
I feel it with my hand, I put my cheek against it.
Nevertheless, I feel there is something between us,
something that keeps me far from the real wall,
for the red color and the sun. There is something
that keeps me in Plato's world of ideas
until my blood begins to throb and the sun sets,
the red wall turns black and cold in the darkness
and crocuses under my window wither.
Transcience engraves new inscriptions into my self
as if I were an old churchbell. The voice
grows clearer and clearer and is heard farther than ever
over walls, over throbbing blood, over the world of ideas
and from beyond its borders a blowing wind
carries the saffron aroma of black crocuses.

N<small>O ONE CAN PUT ME BACK TOGETHER AGAIN</small>
fingering broken tongues you thought perhaps of something else
all cells and scales are silent, ready to answer to questions
which see through, come through, us, objects, fields, rays
which are united by nothing other than truth, the empty word,
                               the sea, the ocean
where we were constructed, put together by bone, cell by cell,
                               syllable by syllable
is he who writes poetry nightly me
with aching back, with gray hair, with your name,
                       with thought only of you
and you come and stand in my room in my eyes in me
and your hands are warm, salty, most beloved
hands which wipe the dust from old letters
                               for the knowledge that
we have been, we have died, we have been born
                               of the dark people
of whom there are so few words and so many
                           graves' heavy stones
that he who rests would have peace on the ash
                   and on the splinters of bone, what, what
were you thinking, girl opening the doors of the promontory
                       with the keys of fairy tales
and asking me for the palmar lines of the megaliths
what were you thinking, Love, fingering my broken fingers
                               by candlelight

AND WHEN THE SEA retreats from here before or after
                    the splitting of the personality

we may still go to be there, to step in the sandpiper's tracks

remain in the wind, remain in the rain in the summer
                              and winter in freedom

because another you and I do not exist and the horizon remains
                    always behind the horizon

to share all the bread that remains, the joy, the snow
                    which does not preserve or forbid

the sun's turning around the equinoctial dark apple
                              trees in gardens

for you, for me, for me who half this life has twined rope
                    and performed under someone's name

trusted flags and entropy plucked out dead nettles

dreaming of wings, wings,

who stands with eyes wide open in a colored room
                              which you tied

from my fingers with your fingers into one

NIGHT COMES and extinguishes the numbers and the year
lifts us from the past and brings away
from the checkerboard table from among kings
                                    queens and knights
the wind's silence and the source the seventh witness
which is a tiny beginning, roots, our infinite roots
wakening still sleeping still in stone crevices in soil
without knowing oneself even without understanding who he is
                              who is woven into them
through the dark earth thus the trees meet all at once
    in the upper and lower world through mother's mute flesh
fingers with fingers, leaves with leaves, loins with loins,
silently blood and earth fall from between us
your young body bursts into flames under dry leaves

ELDER-TREES that thrushes have sown
near St. Peter's cemetery under the precipice
are bigger and more abundantly flowered
than last year. Some steps farther,
the ruins of a burnt house
are vanishing under burdock and nettles.
In the garden there are always the same
leafless trees – a willow and some apple trees
I tried to draw a year ago
when it was spring, as now, and my mother
was dying in the hospital. The gulls shriek
and boats drone farther up the river.
And in the bushes near the old dump,
the nightingales continue to sing the same
"lazy girl, lazy girl, where's the whip, where's the whip"
as though they had learned nothing
and forgotten nothing.

ONCE I GOT A POSTCARD from the Fiji Islands
with a picture of sugar cane harvest. Then I realized
that nothing at all is exotic in itself.
There is no difference between digging potatoes
                              in our Mutiku garden
and sugar cane harvesting in Viti Levu.
Everything that is is very ordinary
or, rather, neither ordinary nor strange.
Far-off lands and foreign peoples are a dream,
a dreaming with open eyes
somebody does not wake from.
It's the same with poetry – seen from afar
it's something special, mysterious, festive.
No, poetry is even less
special than a sugar cane plantation or potato field.
Poetry is like sawdust coming from under the saw
or soft yellowish shavings from a plane.
Poetry is washing hands in the evening
or a clean handkerchief that my late aunt
never forgot to put in my pocket.

Potatoes are dug, ash trees yellow,
sunflower seeds, ripe apples rotting
under the apple tree – as always,
we have more works than days and something
is always left unharvested, unpicked, unfinished.
The plot has to be dug, the fence needs mending –
then we can go, the sky overcast.
Soon, the leaves will be fallen, soon
the essence of things will be more clearly visible:
the black bare twigs of a lowland birch swaying
on the horizon of a gray twilit sky.

PART

V

KARL BARTH, Paul Tillich, Karl Rahner.
Some more immortals with two-thousand-year-old peaches
and volumes of collected works
somewhere on the Western Mountains.
Theology never dies. Blue smoke thickens
into new ghosts, letters, books, commentaries,
snails, seaweed, sponges. Hour by hour
thickens the half-living crust
on the oaken board-planks
and the cheeks of the sails get wrinkled and sooty,
longing for open seas and fresh winds,
smells and colors of foreign lands:
cedar of Lebanon, balm of Gilead,
silk of China and girls of the South, singing
in strange tongues and looking strangely
without fear and shame into your eyes, through your eyes,
through ourselves. Foreign girls
with light steps and tiny silver bells
on their hips and sleeves.
But if I had no love I would be a

kymbalon alalazon
alalazon
alala
lala
la

SHUNRYU SUZUKI
a little Japanese living
and teaching in California
couldn't be my teacher
one of my non-teachers
a little lit match from God's matchbox
sea wind soon blew out
somewhere between California and Estonia
somewhere between East and West
between somewhere and nowhere
nobody can find out what remained of him
after the wind has blown and the tide
come and gone – the white sand
as smooth as before – but his smile
from the back cover of *Zen Mind Beginner's Mind*
has silently infected book after book on my shelves
and perhaps shelves themselves and walls and wallpapers too

COMING HOME.
Three kilometers along the bank of the frozen river.
Only some open spots left.
Dozens of ducks quacking, swimming, splashing,
diving their heads into the icy water
and shaking them.
Some people standing on the bridge,
throwing them crumbs of bread.
Some lanterns in the dusk
and snow falling falling
silently, softly, and in this silence
suddenly a voice calling us,
reminding us there is something that is
more even than life. Silence. Beauty.
Falling snow. Perfect crystals. Flakes.
Harmony. Beauty. *To kalon.*
Snowflakes become drops of water
on my face. In my beard.
Sound of water buried, shut
in the silence of snow. Voice
of God. More even than God.
Snowflakes. Voice of Water. *Mizu no oto.*
Vox aquae. Vox Dei.

OM SVABHAVASUDDAH SARVA DHARMAH. No selfhood.
Everything without own-being, without selfhood.
No self. No own. No hood.
No ness. No ism. No tion. No thing.
All melting away, water trickling
from the roof, from the icicles.
Water drip-dropping. Winter's heart broken.
Winter's eyes wet. Some mountains
are mountains again. Some rivers are rivers again.
Some universals are real. Universalia sunt realia.
Some are not. Realia non sunt realia.
Icicles melting. Water dripping. You can
take one of them and put it in your mouth.
No smell. No taste. No color. Pure ice
melting into pure water.
One into another. One into itself.
No self. No own. No ness. No thing.
One in one. One in all. All in one.
Spring sky in a falling drop.
Li Po in a Seteria grain. Universe in a grain of sand.
All in all. River river again.
No self. Water again water. Drip. Drop.

AFTERWORD

Some poets have careers in poetry. Others have lives in it. Jaan Kap-
linski certainly belongs among the latter. In our correspondence over
the past years, his letters reveal a man of modesty and intelligence in
many ways naive regarding the ways of the West. In one recent letter,
he says, "Some of my international friends have tried to organize an
article about [*The Same Sea in Us All*] for the New York Review of
Books. You know, I do not understand what publicity and public
relations really mean in the USA, and I probably tend to underesti-
mate them. So I do not feel interested in such things. But people say it
is all-important, that one must be introduced into the literary world
in this way. Let it be so. Sometimes I am perhaps afraid to lose my
soul in this way. Do not think it is not easy to lose it here. It is.
Sometimes I think it would be interesting to live in a world where
there would be no public cultural life. To live on a solitary island with
your family or in some little group of like-minded people. What
would be the goals and values there? What kind of poems or litera-
ture would we create? We are looking all the time towards our big,
anonymous . . . and weary audience. We are not creating, thinking,
writing for our nearest, for our children, for our friends. . . ."

As is so often the case with Kaplinski, what begins in apparent
naiveté concludes in wisdom. His concerns are those of poets since
the beginning of rime – seasons, family life, attention to daily detail,

and wisdom enough to know that posterity and fame are illusions, distractions from the real work.

In another letter, he told me of an old philologist who studied French for many years until he finally retired to visit France, but couldn't understand a word until he found a sailor who spoke in a poor Scandinavian. Kaplinski, who translates Latin, Greek, Romance languages, Polish, Lithuanian, classical Chinese and more, also observed that upon hearing colloquial American jokes, he couldn't understand the humor, adding, "I couldn't get around in one of your supermarkets very well."

His poems are written in colloquial Estonian, "the working language of our high schools." But he asks to "de-emphasize" his role as a national poet: "I do not consider it right to be called primarily the poet of the oppressed Estonian people. I think my background is larger. If I write about Estonians, I mean Estonians; but if I write about Indians, I mean Indians. And in a sense, I am an Indian too. I am a Buddhist, and I am simply a man. And, primarily, first of all, a sentient being, a sensitive being. And my poetry is a poetry written by such a being, not simply by an Estonian."

It is at once frightening and heart-warming to realize just how very much more Jaan Kaplinski knows about life and history on the west coast of the United States than we know about life anywhere in the Soviet Union. I sent a few books to him and was thanked months later with insightful comments on the poetry of Gary Snyder, Kenneth Rexroth, and recent poems of my own. I, on the other hand, couldn't get through a good Kaplinski poem even with a dictionary without someone along to act as guide and tutor.

"Sympathy to those who are like you and to those who are unlike you," Kaplinski says. "Our lives have been so different, but our poems aren't? I think so."

Some poets make a career of poesy. For others, poetry makes the life. Kaplinski, his wife, and five children winter in a small flat and spend their summers at a small country home "visited only by titmice and hares which love the apple trees." His is a poetry of the diurnal and the seasonal, a poetry of domesticity and enormous compassion. In the economy of the soul, thrift is ruinous. His poems are testimony to the silence of wisdom, the infinitely gentle whisper of genuine affection, informed by compassionate revelation, that most rare and startling attribute of poetry which Robert Duncan named "evidence of the real."

Our lives, so alike and yet so unalike, cross the barriers of language and politics and religion, and intertwine. We share an interest in Li Po and Tu Fu, in Tranströmer and Bo Carpelan. We each practice a kind of Ch'an discipline. I believe the poet would not be offended if I called us *unsui,* beginners, because, as Odysseas Elytis says, everything we love is always beginning. When we begin to enter into the real world, the borders, which have always wandered, suddenly vanish.

This is the second time I have served as midwife to a volume of Jaan Kaplinski's poems in English, more editor than translator. It is an honor I cherish, and in the doing, an act of devotion. Thanks from both of us to my revered editor at Breitenbush Books, James Anderson, who published *The Same Sea in Us All* in 1985. Thanks also to Riina Tamm, my patient and generous co-respondent in all matters Estonian. There are no words with which to thank Tree Swenson for her fifteen years as publisher and guiding light at Copper Canyon Press: nine bows.

Most of all, thanks are due to Jaan Kaplinski, poet. And citizen of the world.

SAM HAMILL

The cover image, "Inclosure, White," is by
George Tsutakawa (sumi on washi, 39″ × 34″, 1986),
courtesy of the artist and Foster-White Gallery.
(Photograph by Robert Vinnedge.)

The type is Sabon, with Weiss display, and was
set by Fjord Press Typography.

Book design by Tree Swenson.